PROPERTY OF

ISBN 978-1-4521-1966-3

MIX
Paper from
responsible sources
FSC® C008047

Manufactured in China

Design by EMILY DUBIN

Chronicle Books publishes distinctive books and gifts.
From award-winning children's titles, bestselling cook-
books, and eclectic pop culture to acclaimed works
of art and design, stationery, and journals, we craft
publishing that's instantly recognizable for its spirit
and creativity. Enjoy our publishing and become part
of our community at www.chroniclebooks.com.

10 9 8 7 6 5 4 3 2

CHRONICLE BOOKS
680 SECOND STREET
SAN FRANCISCO, CA 94107
WWW.CHRONICLEBOOKS.COM